MARIO ANDRETTI

Photo Album

World Champion Driver Series

Peter Nygaard

Iconografix
Photo Album Series

Iconografix
PO Box 446
Hudson, Wisconsin 54016 USA

Library of Congress Card Number: 99-71754

ISBN 1-58388-009-7

99 00 01 02 03 04 05 5 4 3 2 1

Printed in the United States of America

Cover and book design by Shawn Glidden

Edited by Dylan Frautschi

Iconografix Inc. exists to preserve history through the publication of notable photographic archives and the list of titles under the Iconografix imprint is constantly growing. Transportation enthusiasts should be on the Iconografix mailing list and are invited to write and ask for a catalog, free of charge.

Authors and editors in the field of transportation history are invited to contact the Editorial Department at Iconografix, Inc., PO Box 446, Hudson, WI 54016. We require a minimum of 120 photographs per subject. We prefer subjects narrow in focus, e.g., a specific model, railroad, or racing venue. Photographs must be of high-quality, suited to large format reproduction.

Mario Andretti

Mario Andretti: The Great All-rounder

This book about Mario Andretti is part of a series of Photo Albums on Formula One World Champions. It therefore concentrates on Mario's Formula One career, which, even though it began in 1968 and ended in 1982, only included five full seasons. That he still managed to win the 1978 title proves what a great driver Mario was, but the statistics also reveal that Mario was far more than a Formula One driver. Unlike almost all other World Champions who concentrated solely on Formula One, Mario was racing here, there and everywhere. As an all-rounder, Mario Andretti is surely the greatest racing driver ever - no one ever participated in more forms of motor racing for as long or as successfully as the tough, little American.

Mario Gabriele Andretti is one of twin brothers born on February 28, 1940 to a farming family in the Italian town of Montona near Trieste. After the war, the area where the Andrettis lived became a part of Yugoslavia, and their comfortable life changed dramatically. "Suddenly Communism arrived - all that stuff about everybody being equal. Sure we were all equal - we all had nothing!" Mario has said about the difficult time, which saw the family move to a displaced person's camp in Lucca near Pisa in 1948 - and Mario develop a healthy dislike of Communism. In Lucca, where several families often lived in the same room, Mario and his twin brother Aldo, developed an interest for cars - at first parking cars for a local garage owner and later riding a 175 ccm MV motorcycle and even trying out a small Formula Junior car. One year, the garage owner took the racing mad Andretti boys to both the Mille Miglia road race and the Grand Prix at Monza, and Mario and Aldo were immediately hooked. Mario became a fan of the 1952-1953 World Champion Alberto Ascari, and even though he never actually met the great Italian, Mario claims Ascari had a greater influence on his life than anybody else.

In 1955, Papa Andretti brought his family to Nazareth, Pennsylvania where his wife had relatives, and shortly after settling in the States, the twins relaunched their racing career at the local speedway but "forgot" to tell their family. The twins took turns behind the wheel of their much-modified Hudson Hornet, and at the time it seemed that Aldo was the fastest Andretti. Aldo and Mario both won their first two races but in Aldo's third race, at Hatfield, he crashed and fractured his skull so badly that he was in a coma for a week. Mario, at first trying to convince his parents that Aldo had injured himself falling from a truck while watching the race, eventually had to tell the truth when police threatened to contact the Andretti home. When Aldo finally woke up, legend has it that his first words to Mario were: "Considering everything, I am sure glad you were the guy who had to tell Papa!"

Papa Andretti didn't talk to his boys for quite a while after the accident, and even though he tried racing again several times, Aldo was never as fast as before the shunt, and the twins eventually drifted apart with Aldo marrying and moving to Indianapolis for a career in the tire business.

Mario continued in racing, and from modified and stock car racing he moved into sprint cars and, in 1964, ChampCar racing in the USAC championship. Here, it took Mario less than four minutes to become a super star of US racing - 3 minutes, 46 seconds and 63/00 to be exact: This is Mario's practice time for his first Indy 500 in 1965 - a time fast enough to beat the lap record and give him pole position after the first qualifying day. In the race, the 25 year old rookie drove like a veteran and ran with the leaders for most of the day; eventually finishing third.

Several wins and three titles within the next five years saw Mario firmly establish himself in the ChampCar world, but he also raced successfully in Sports Cars, winning the 1967 Sebring 12 Hour race, and when he entered probably the most specialized form of US racing, NASCAR, he promptly won the 1967 Daytona 500!

European racing bosses became interested in the versatile American, and Colin Chapman of Lotus offered Mario a Formula One Lotus 49B for the Italian and US Grands Prix at the end of 1968. Mario created a sensation at Monza. He was fastest in testing in the week leading up to the race, and he was again fastest in Friday morning's opening practice, but then left for the Hoosier Hundred race in the USA on Saturday. After Saturday's qualifying in Monza, held in cooler and thus faster conditions, Mario's time was still good enough for 10th place on the grid, but when he returned to Italy, he was not allowed to start the Grand Prix as he had competed in another race within 24 hours. The Formula One regulars were not too unhappy with the decision to ban the fast American from the race, but four weeks later Mario was back - this time for the American Grand Prix at Watkins Glen. Incredibly, he was again the fastest. He started from pole position and ran second in the opening stages, but probably the most sensational Formula One debut in Grand Prix history ended after only 32 laps when the Lotus developed clutch problems.

The next four years saw Mario compete sporadically in Formula One while having a full-time program in the USA. In his third Formula One Grand Prix, the South African Grand Prix in 1969 and again in a Lotus 49B, he was catching the leaders when he retired from third place. Two more 1969 Grands Prix for Lotus, this time in the experimental 63 4wd model, did not bring any success, but at least Mario managed to win the Indy 500 in the US. He dominated proceedings at the Speedway for most of May in his Lotus 64 4wd, but an accident, caused by a broken hub, destroyed the car and left Mario with facial burns. He switched to his back-up car, a Hawke, and still managed to take a comfortable win in the race.

STP, which had sponsored the 1969 Indy 500 program, established a Formula One team for Mario in 1970, using a chassis from the new March organization. Still a part-time program, the 1970 Formula One season was not a great success, but Mario finally managed to score his first Formula One point when he finished a distant third in the tough Spanish Grand Prix - which was also his first Grand Prix finish ever.

For 1971, Mario signed with Ferrari for both Formula One and the World Sports Car Championship. For an Italian with Ascari as his hero, it must have been a dream come true, and Mario's Formula One career with the Prancing Horse had a great start when he won his first Formula One race of 1971, the South African Grand Prix at Kyalami. In his next Formula One race for Ferrari, the non-championship US West Grand Prix at Ontario, Mario was also first across the line, but the remaining four Grands Prix on his 1971 program only brought a fourth place on the Nürburgring.

Why did Mario not concentrate on Formula One when it was obvious he would be in with a chance of the championship if only he agreed to a full-time program? Mario said he had commitments to Firestone Tyre Company - commitments which centered on American racing as the tire company had other drivers contracted for Formula One. "There isn't much security in this business and the Firestone contract represented a lot to me," the street-wise American explained at the time.

Mario's second year with Ferrari, 1972, was not a success in Formula One, but the great American all-rounder took several wins for the Prancing Horse in the World Sports Car Championship.

Mario did not compete in Formula One in 1973 and for most of 1974, but the Vel's Parnelli Jones team was busy building a Formula One car for Mario for 1975. Mario prepared for his Formula One comeback in various US series; actually winning the USAC Dirt Track Championship(!) before entering the final two Grands Prix of 1974. The Vel's Parnelli Jones organization was never 100 percent committed to the Formula One program, and the high point was the Spanish Grand Prix of 1975 which Mario led before crashing out. The Vel's Parnelli Jones Formula One team collapsed after only two races in 1976, and a furious Mario had to look elsewhere for a Formula One drive.

Lotus had just experienced their worst season ever, and a marriage of convenience was the logical solution for Mario and Lotus boss Colin Chapman. At first, things did not exactly look great, but hard work from Lotus and Mario's talent as a development driver eventually made the Lotus 77 competitive, and Mario finished the 1976 season with pole position and a win in the Japanese Grand Prix.

The 1977 Lotus 78 was even better, introducing the "wing-car" concept in Formula One, and Mario won more races than any other driver. However, engine problems in four races in a row in the second part of the season cost him all chances of the championship, but in 1978, with the dominant Lotus 79, Mario finally took the title as only the second American after Phil Hill in 1961. Mario and his teammate, Sweden's Ronnie Peterson, were in a class of their own, and the Swede was a loyal back-up for the American. It was actually in Peterson's contract that he had to support Mario's championship aspirations, and when the Swede on occasions proved the faster of the two Lotus drivers, it created controversy - but only outside the team. Ronnie Peterson accepted his position with grace and loyalty, and Colin Chapman underlined that Mario deserved the championship. "Mario's contribution to the competitiveness of the Lotus 79 was immense - without him it would have been a different car. Frankly, Mario has made Team Lotus what it is today," Chapman said after Mario had won the championship. He continued, "There were those who said that Mario was winning races only because Peterson was allowing him to do so. Ronnie was a very great racing driver, one of the best I have ever seen, but he owed a lot to Mario - and he knew it."

Mario Andretti clinched the title in the Italian Grand Prix at Monza. It should have been the happiest day in Mario's career but turned into a tragedy when friend and teammate Ronnie Peterson was involved in a multiple accident just after the start. His Lotus burst into flames, and he had to be rescued from the wreckage by his colleagues. The first bulletins from the hospital spoke of severe leg injuries but also claimed that a full recovery was possible, but Peterson's conditions deteriorated during the night, and on Monday morning - Mario's first day as Formula One World Champion - he died. "Unfortunately, motor racing is also like this," was all Mario could say when he came to the hospital early on Monday morning.

Mario stayed with Lotus for two more Formula One seasons, but the Lotus 80 of 1979, designed to be the "Next Step," was a fiasco and the Lotus 81 of 1980 was neither reliable nor competitive. For 1981, Mario's final, full Formula One season, he signed with Alfa Romeo, but three points for fourth place in the opening race, the US West Grand Prix in Long Beach, was poor reward for a frustrating season.

The year 1982 saw Mario return to US racing full-time, but he still competed in three Grands Prix. Williams invited him to stand-in for the suddenly retired Carlos Reutemann in the US West Grand Prix, and he made an emotional come-back for Ferrari at the Italian Grand Prix at Monza as stand-in for the injured Didier Pironi. At Monza, where he had seen his great idol Alberto Ascari race in the early 1950s, stunned the Formula One world on his debut for Lotus in 1968 and won his World Championship on the day his teammate Peterson crashed fatally, a 42 year old Mario proved that he could still be competitive in the right equipment. Sensationally, he qualified on pole position, and for the Italian Tifosi, who had lost their idol Gilles Villeneuve in a tragic accident earlier in the season, "The Man from Nazareth" had truly come home. Mario finished third in the race - a position which clinched the Constructor's World Championship for Ferrari - and his great but often sporadic Formula One

career came to an end when he retired from the US Grand Prix in Las Vegas a few weeks later.

Mario returned to ChampCar racing in the States, won the 1984 Championship and took his final ChampCar win at the age of 53 years - the oldest race winner in ChampCar history - at Phoenix in 1993. By then, his son Michael was a front-runner in ChampCar racing, winning the ChampCar title in 1991 and making his Formula One debut in 1993 with McLaren. After a difficult debut season in Formula One, Michael returned to the States in 1994 and rejoined Mario in ChampCar racing.

For Mario, the 1994 season was officially titled the "Arriverdeci, Mario" Tour, and he retired from ChampCar at the end of the season having scored a podium finish in Phoenix.

It wasn't the end of Mario's career, though. He continued in sports-prototypes, trying to win the Le Mans 24 Hour. After Indy 500, Daytona 500, Sebring 12 Hour and the Formula One World Championship, Le Mans was arguably the only "classic" not on Mario's racing C.V., and he often entered the 24 Hour race with his son Michael, and even created an Andretti-Andretti-Andretti entry in 1988 when nephew John joined Mario and Michael in a Porsche 962C, which finished sixth.

Mario came close to winning the French 24 Hour race in 1995 when he finished second in a Courage-Porsche. Having crashed out of Le Mans 1997, it seemed that Mario's career was finally over. Today he follows his son Michael's ChampCar career from the pit and enjoys family life with his wife Dee Ann, a girl who was supposed to improve Mario's English shortly after arriving in the USA and ended up as Mrs. Andretti in 1961.

It is a comfortable life for the Andretti family. Motor racing has made Mario a very rich man indeed. His total prize money earnings from ChampCar racing totals more than 10 million dollars, and this is just a fraction of his income from one of the longest and most successful careers in international racing.

But his happy face when he climbed aboard yet another new car and his bubbling enthusiasm for anything connected to racing and speed reveal that he didn't do it for the money: The man who has been called the "Most Professional Racing Driver Ever" would probably have done it all for free...

Part One:
Mario Andretti's
Formula One Career

Mario Andretti made his Formula One debut at Monza in 1968. Lotus boss Colin Chapman invited the versatile American to try one of the team's Lotus 49Bs, and Mario was sensationally fastest in the opening practice session, but then flew to the USA for a ChampCar race. On his return to Monza, he was not allowed to start the race.

Mario Andretti at Monza 1968 for his Formula One debut. Before entering Formula One, Mario had won two ChampCar titles in the United States, and the American series was to remain his main priority for several years: Despite making his debut in 1968, Mario's first, full Formula One campaign was actually the 1977 season.

Jackie Stewart (left) and reigning World Champion Dennis Hulme (second from right) welcome Americans Mario Andretti and Bobby Unser (right) to Formula One at Monza in 1968. The Americans went back to the States after the opening practice session, and were not allowed to start the race on their return to Monza.

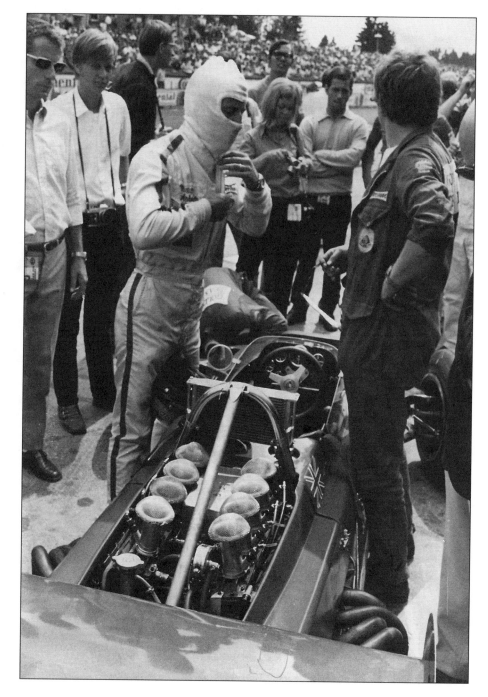

Mario stayed with Lotus for a limited Formula One campaign in 1969. He started the season with the South African Grand Prix in the Lotus 49B, but switched to the 63 4wd for the German and US Grands Prix. Photo shows Mario preparing for the German Grand Prix at the Nürburgring; a race which saw the American start 15th, only to crash out.

The Lotus 63 4wd, which Mario prepares to take out for the German Grand Prix 1969, was never a success in Formula One, as the car was both over-weight and over-complicated. However, Mario put his skills as a test and development driver to good use, and Lotus' 4wd was also used in the American ChampCar series.

Mario in the Lotus 63 4wd during practice for the German Grand Prix at the Nürburgring in 1969. It was Mario's first race at the awesome Nürburgring, and he qualified the difficult 4wd car 15th fastest among 25 cars. In the race he lost control on the opening lap and crashed out at the Wippermann section, but escaped unhurt.

Mario was an established ChampCar star in the States in the late sixties, having won the championship twice and the Indy 500 in 1969 (when he also went on to win the ChampCar title for a third time). In Formula One, he was only racing sporadically for Lotus - here he is preparing for his third and final race of 1969, the American Grand Prix.

The STP Corporation, the sponsor of Mario's ChampCar program, established a Formula One team for 1970. The chassis came from new Formula One car manufacturer, March, which supplied several teams in 1970. The March was never truly competitive - just look at Mario's irresolute face before the start of the Spanish Grand Prix.

The 1970 Spanish Grand Prix was a tough race with several retirements. A crash between Jacky Ickx (Ferrari) and Jackie Oliver (BRM) saw both cars burn out at the track side, but the race was not stopped. Mario, here passing the scene of the accident, finished third, but was more than a lap behind the winner, Jackie Stewart.

The Spanish Grand Prix 1970 was Mario's sixth Formula One Grand Prix and his first finish - in a somewhat lucky third place. Here, Mario's March is attacked by French driver Henri Pescarolo in a Matra. The Frenchman retired from the race with engine problems while Mario went on to take his first points in the Formula One World Championship.

In 1970 only Ferrari, BRM and Matra built their own engines in Formula One - all other cars, including Mario's STP March, used the Ford Cosworth V-8. A shortage of engines made life tough for Mario, who is here seen waiting for the start of the British Grand Prix at Brands Hatch. He retired from the race due to rear suspension problems.

For 1971, Mario signed with Ferrari for both Formula One and sports cars. The program got off to a great start when Mario won his debut race for the "Prancing Horse", the South African Grand Prix at Kyalami. The American had qualified in fourth position, and on his way to his first Grand Prix win, Mario also posted fastest lap.

Mario in a Ferrari 312B leading John Surtees in a Surtees-Ford during the South African Grand Prix 1971; a race which saw the American score his first Grand Prix win. He went on to win the non-championship US Grand Prix West in Ontario a few weeks later, but for the rest of the 1971 Formula One season he only raced sporadically for Ferrari.

Having won his first two Formula One races for Ferrari, Mario had a difficult third race. In the Spanish Grand Prix he qualified eighth and retired with fuel pump problems. In the following race, things went from bad to worse when he failed to qualify in Monte Carlo because technical problems forced him to miss the only dry session.

Apart from his win in the South African Grand Prix, Mario only scored three more points in the 1971 Formula One World Championship, with fourth place in the German Grand Prix at the Nürburgring. The photo shows Mario (number 5) under pressure from Francois Cevert in a Tyrrell-Ford. The Frenchman went on to finish second.

Mario never scored any podium finishes at the legendary Nürburgring, probably the most difficult and dangerous circuit in Formula One in the early 1970s. Photo shows Mario, his Ferrari almost airborne, in the 1971 German Grand Prix, which was won by Jackie Stewart (Tyrrell-Ford) ahead of teammate Francois Cevert and Ferrari's Clay Regazzoni.

Mario stayed with Ferrari for the 1972 Formula One season - but still only for a sporadic program. His first race was the season-opener; the Argentine Grand Prix in Buenos Aires. By now, he was driving the 312B2, which replaced the 312B midway through the 1971 season. Mario retired from the Argentine race with engine problems.

For the second Grand Prix of 1972, on South Africa's Kyalami circuit, Ferrari tried a new "wide nose" front. The new front-end aerodynamics suited the Kyalami circuit, and Mario (pictured) qualified sixth and finished fourth. However, for the next Grand Prix in Spain, Ferrari reverted to the original front-end design with two, smaller front wings.

After another sporadic Formula One season in 1972, Mario decided to concentrate on his American programs in 1973 and 1974. However, his ChampCar team, Vel's Parnelli Jones Racing, was about to enter Formula One, and Mario made a comeback at the end of the 1974 season with two Grands Prix in Parnelli's new Formula One car.

Vel's Parnelli Jones' Formula One team was never a great success - budgets were limited and interest divided between Formula One and the American ChampCar series. Despite the difficult conditions, Mario drove as well as ever and was actually leading the Spanish Grand Prix at Montjuich Park (photo) until he crashed out.

Mario scored Vel's Parnelli Jones' first points in the Formula One World Championship with a fine fourth place in the Swedish Grand Prix in Anderstorp (photo). In the following race, at France's Paul Ricard circuit, Mario finished fifth. Thereafter, the car was not competitive again until the final Grand Prix in the USA, but here Mario retired.

Vel's Parnelli Jones' Formula One car, seen here between practice sessions for the Swedish Grand Prix at Anderstorp in 1975, was designed by ex-Lotus man Maurice Philippe. It was a conventional design using the by now almost universal Ford Cosworth V-8 engine, a Hewland gearbox and Goodyear tires.

Vel's Parnelli Jones' did not enter the first two 1976 Grands Prix in Argentina and Brazil. For these races, Mario went back to Lotus, which had just introduced the new 77-model. It was a difficult car, but Mario still managed to qualify third for the Brazilian Grand Prix at Interlagos (photo), but he retired from the race with ignition problems.

"Now listen, young boy - it is done like this." During the 1976 season, Stirling Moss (left) worked as a commentator in Formula One, and the Englishman - generally regarded as the best driver never to win the World Championship in Formula One - is here seen explaining a few things to Mario before the Swedish Grand Prix at Anderstorp.

Mario relaxing with 1972-1974 World Champion Emerson Fittipaldi and Lotus teammate Gunnar Nilsson at Anderstorp during the Swedish Grand Prix weekend in 1976. The Swedish circuit suited the Lotus, and for the first time since his sensational debut at Watkins Glen in 1968, Mario qualified on the front row - next to Jody Scheckter on pole.

After only two 1976 Grands Prix Vel's Parnelli Jones closed their Formula One team, and Mario went back to Lotus - again. The Lotus 77 was gradually improved, and Mario qualified third for the British Grand Prix (photo). In the race he retired with engine problems, but the writing was on the wall: Lotus - and Mario - were back.

The hard development work with the Lotus 77 was finally rewarded at the final Grand Prix of 1976 at Fuji in Japan. Mario, seen climbing into the car for practice, took pole position and won the race. To the left of the car is Peter Warr (with glasses), the Lotus team manager, and Colin Chapman's right hand man in the team.

Mario and his second driver at Lotus in 1976-1977; Sweden's Gunnar Nilsson (right), celebrating Mario's win in the 1976 Japanese Grand Prix with local beauties. Nilsson learned a lot from the experienced American, but just as he was ready to join the new Arrows team as team leader in 1978, he developed cancer. He died in late 1978.

At the end of the 1976 season, Mario (with back to camera) invited Gunnar Nilsson (left) and Ronnie Peterson (right), who had both been his teammates at Lotus during the season, to his home in Nazareth. Swedish racing journalist Frederik Af Petersens also joined the party, which flew into Nazareth in Mario's personal plane (background).

For the 1977 season, Colin Chapman created the Lotus 78; the first "wing car" in Formula One. A specially designed bottom and the long side pods beside the cockpit created a lot of downforce, and Mario, here testing the car before the season, suddenly had the best car in field for the first time in his Formula One career.

The Lotus 78 made its debut in the opening Grand Prix of 1978, held at the Buenos Aires Autodromo in Argentina. Mario only qualified the new Lotus in eighth place and was classified fifth, even though he retired a couple of laps from the end due to a broken rear wheel bearing. Still, all the Lotus 78 needed was a little development.

In the South African Grand Prix at Kyalami, the third round of the 1977 World Championship, Mario qualified sixth, but retired in the race following a collision with Carlos Reutemann (Ferrari). With testing and development, the Lotus 78 was gradually moving closer and closer to the front of the field, and was soon to be the pace-setter of 1977.

Don't look so worried: Mario (right), Gunnar Nilsson (center), and Lotus technicians (in black uniforms), Tony Southgate (left) and Nigel Bennett during practice for the 1977 US West Grand Prix in Long Beach. Mario qualified second and went on to win the race; his first win of the 1977 season. Nilsson in the other Lotus finished a distant eighth.

The fifth round of the 1977 World Championship was the Spanish Grand Prix at the Jarama circuit. Mario took pole position and won the race in front of Carlos Reutemann (Ferrari) and Jody Scheckter (Wolf). By now it was clear that Colin Chapman had taken the "Next Step" with his wing car design, and Mario was second in the World Championship.

Mario chatting to South Africa's Jody Scheckter before the 1977 Swedish Grand Prix. At this stage of the season, just before the halfway mark, Scheckter, driving a Wolf-Ford, was leading the World Championship three points ahead of Mario. Interestingly, Scheckter's Wolf team was managed by ex-Lotus' team manager Peter Warr.

Mario in the 1977 Swedish Grand Prix at Anderstorp. The American is seen passing the pits, which at Anderstorp was placed a long way from the start and finish, in front of Great Britain's Ruper Keegan in a Hesketh and local hero Ronnie Peterson in the Tyrrel P34 six-wheeler. Peterson was to become Mario's teammate at Lotus in 1978.

Mario was on his way to another dominant win in the 1977 Swedish Grand Prix when he had to go into the pits for extra fuel a few laps from the end. The unscheduled pit stop put him back to sixth place - and it gave France's Jacques Laffite and the Ligier team their first, somewhat lucky Grand Prix win.

Mario in the 1977 French Grand Prix at the Dijon-Prenois circuit. The American took his third pole position in a row at Dijon-Prenois and went on to win the race ahead of John Watson (Brabham-Alfa Romeo) and James Hunt (McLaren-Ford). It was Mario's third win of the season, and it promoted him to second place in the championship.

Mario celebrating his win in the 1977 French Grand Prix at Dijon-Prenois. The American started from pole but lost the lead to James Hunt at the start. It only took Mario four laps to pass the Englishman, and he led all the way to the finish. James Hunt eventually finished third, losing second place to John Watson (right) on lap 16.

Mario leading teammate Gunnar Nilsson during the 1977 British Grand Prix at Silverstone. For Nilsson, in his second and last Grand Prix season before dying from cancer at the end of 1978, it was the perfect position. The young Swede learned a lot from the experienced American during their two seasons together in the Lotus team.

Lotus boss Colin Chapman watches over mechanics adjusting Mario's Lotus 78 during practice for the 1977 British Grand Prix. Chapman was one of the most innovative designers in the history of Formula One, but his ideas were sometimes ahead of the time. The 1977 Lotus 78 was one of Chapman's greatest cars - it took Mario to four Grand Prix wins.

The 1977 British Grand Prix at Silverstone was the start of a bad summer for Mario and Team Lotus. Despite having the fastest car in the field, engine problems too often cost them what looked like certain victories. Here Mario retires at Silverstone a few laps from the end of the race - he also retired with engine problems in the next three races.

Lotus boss Colin Chapman and Mario Andretti talking in the pit during practice for the 1977 Dutch Grand Prix. Chapman had given Mario his first Formula One chance back in 1968, and when they joined forces again in 1976 they were both down. It took the combined genius of Chapman and Mario less than a year to return to the front.

Mario (right) fighting with James Hunt for the lead of the 1977 Dutch Grand Prix. Hunt, the reigning World Champion, was furious with Mario when the cars collided. "We don't overtake on the outside in Formula One," an angry Hunt said. "Well - I got news for you," Mario replied. "As a racer I try to overtake on the outside if I am blocked on the inside!"

Proving a point: Mario (right) lines up to pass Niki Lauda's Ferrari on the outside in the 1977 Dutch Grand Prix. Mario's race ended with a broken engine, and Lauda went on to win the race. Lauda only won three Grands Prix to Mario's four during 1977, but his Ferrari was more reliable than the Lotus, and the Austrian took the championship.

Mario Andretti during the 1977 Italian Grand Prix at Monza. For this race, Mario qualified only fourth fastest behind James Hunt (McLaren), Carlos Reutemann (Ferrari) and Jody Scheckter (Wolf). The American was third at the end of lap one, second at the end of lap two, and took the lead on lap nine and led all the way to the finish.

Colin Chapman (center) and his Dream Team for 1978. Mario (left) and Sweden's Ronnie Peterson with the Lotus 79, which was to become the superior car of 1978. Peterson re-joined Lotus on the clear understanding that he was to help Mario win the World Championship, and the Swede proved totally loyal all season.

Mario used the Lotus 78 for the first five Grands Prix of 1978, while the Lotus 79 was developed in private tests. The new car finally made its debut in round six, the Belgian Grand Prix at Zolder, and Mario promptly took pole position and won the race. It was his second win of the season as he had won the opening race in Argentina in the Lotus 78.

Mario and Lotus teammate Ronnie Peterson (left) celebrate their one-two win in the 1978 Belgian Grand Prix. While Mario was in the new Lotus 79, Peterson was still driving the Lotus 78 from 1977, but in the next race, at Spain's Jarama circuit outside Madrid, both Lotus drivers were in the superior 79.

In the 1978 Swedish Grand Prix, Mario took his third pole position in a row. By now, the Lotus 79, which refined the "wing car" concept developed by Colin Chapman with the Lotus 78 of 1977, was in a class of its own, and with teammate Ronnie Peterson loyally supporting the American's title aspirations, it was a great summer for Lotus.

Lotus' rivals were left behind by Chapman's "wing car" concept in 1978, and in the Swedish Grand Prix, Brabham tried to fight back with the infamous "fan car." A big fan at the rear "sucked" the car to the track. Niki Lauda in the Brabham, here about to overtake Mario at Anderstorp, won the race, but the car was banned a few days later.

In the 1978 French Grand Prix at Paul Ricard, John Watson in a Brabham (now without the "fan") took pole position, but Mario won the race. The picture, taken early in the race, shows Mario leading Patrick Tambay (McLaren), Niki Lauda (Brabham), James Hunt (McLaren), teammate Ronnie Peterson, Jacques Laffite (Ligier) and Alan Jones (Williams).

The top-three in the 1978 French Grand Prix. It was Mario's fourth Grand Prix win of the season and Lotus' third 1-2 win. Loyal teammate Ronnie Peterson celebrates with Mario and James Hunt (right), who finished third in a McLaren. The controversy about "overtaking on the outside" from the 1977 Dutch Grand Prix was a thing of the past.

"That car is just too fast!" Switzerland's Clay Regazzoni (right) jokes with Mario before practice for the 1978 British Grand Prix at Brands Hatch. The Lotus 79 was superior, and poor Regazzoni, in an uncompetitive Shadow, was usually a couple of seconds per lap slower. Mario and Regazzoni were teammates at Ferrari in 1971-1972.

Mario in the 1978 British Grand Prix. It was a bad weekend for the American as his loyal teammate Ronnie Peterson, on poorer tires, took pole position with Mario only second. In the race, Mario took the lead in front of Peterson, but the Ford Cosworth engine in Mario's Lotus 79 developed problems, and the American retired after 28 laps.

The start of the 1978 Dutch Grand Prix at Zandvoort. As usual in this season, Mario and teammate Ronnie Peterson are in front with the American (left) taking the lead from pole position. The Lotus drivers also led the World Championship, and with another 1-2 win for the "Mario and Ronnie Show" in Holland, this lead was increased.

The final "Mario and Ronnie Show." Mario leads teammate Ronnie Peterson in the 1978 Dutch Grand Prix at Zandvoort. As usual, the Swede was loyal to Mario, but one of the strongest partnership in Grand Prix racing was to end tragically at the next race at Monza, Italy. Peterson crashed shortly after the start and died from his injuries.

As World Champion, it was natural for Mario to stay with Lotus for 1979. Long-time sponsor John Player Special left the team, and during the winter 1978-79, Mario tested the Lotus 79 in this almost totally black livery. Martini joined the team as title sponsor before the start of the season, and the cars were painted dark green.

The Lotus 80, which made its debut in the 1979 Spanish Grand Prix was meant to be the "Next Step" after the successful 77 and 78 designs. However, the latest Lotus was never truly competitive even though Mario (photo) finished third in its debut race in Spain.

Colin Chapman and Mario Andretti gave up on the Lotus 80 midway through the 1979 season and went back to the 1978 79. By now, other teams had developed their own "wing cars," and the Lotus - the pace-setter only the previous season - was suddenly not competitive. Photo shows Chapman and Mario during practice for the Dutch Grand Prix.

Mario in the Lotus 79 during the 1979 Dutch Grand Prix at Zandvoort. For this race, which Lotus had dominated in 1978 with the Lotus 79, Mario only qualified 17th and he retired from the race with rear suspension problems. Photo shows Mario in front of Jody Scheckter (Ferrari) who went on to win the World Championship.

Lotus again changed sponsor for 1980. Martini left the team after only one year and was replaced by oil company Essex. Colin Chapman and his design team produced the new Lotus 81 for the start of the season, and Mario qualified the new car in a promising 6th position for the opening round of the World Championship in Argentina (photo).

Mario in the Lotus 81. Despite a promising grid position in the Argentine Grand Prix, the 1981 Lotus was never truly competitive, and the American did not score any points until the final race of the year; the US Grand Prix at Watkins Glen where he finished sixth. With only one point, it was Mario's worst season since doing only three races in 1969.

Mario in the pits during practice for the 1980 German Grand Prix. The race took place at the high-speed Hockenheim circuit, and in order to compete with the powerful turbo cars, Lotus, still running the normally aspirated Ford Cosworth V-8 engine, took off the front wings in order to gain more top speed on the long straights.

Mario in the front wingless Lotus 81 during the 1980 German Grand Prix. The rear wing was also adjusted for minimum drag on the long Hockenheim straights, but despite this radical, aerodynamic set-up, the American only qualified ninth. In the race, he finished in seventh place - one position from of a World Championship point.

For 1981 Mario signed with Alfa Romeo for Formula One. After a couple of uncompetitive years with Lotus and their Ford Cosworth V-8 the American looked forward to the more powerful Alfa Romeo V-12. The first race of the year was the US West Grand Prix in Long Beach, and here Mario (pictured) qualified sixth and finished in a fine fourth place.

When the Grand Prix circus came to Europe for the main part of the 1981 season, the Alfa Romeo was less competitive. This is Mario in the Belgian Grand Prix at Zolder - he qualified only 18th and finished 10th, one lap behind the winner, in a race plagued by an engine misfire.

1981 saw Mario race for the last time in the famous Monaco Grand Prix in the streets of Monte Carlo. In the big Alfa Romeo, Mario did a good job to qualify 12th, fastest in the field of 31 cars, but in the race he had to retire after a shunt with the young, aggressive Andrea de Cesaris in a McLaren-Ford.

A concentrated Mario before the start of one of the 1981 Grands Prix for Alfa Romeo. Even Mario's abilities as a test and development driver could not make the Alfa Romeo competitive. The Italians had dominated the first two seasons of the Formula One World Championship in 1950 -1951, but only came back to the sport at the end of 1978.

1981 was Mario's last, full season in the Formula One World Championship. Mario wanted to go back to American racing and concentrate on the ChampCar championship. His last Formula One race for Alfa Romeo was the US Las Vegas Grand Prix where he qualified 10th, but retired in the race due to a broken rear suspension.

Mario's retirement from Formula One was short-lived. When Argentina's Carlos Reutemann suddenly retired after only one race of the 1982 season, the front-running Williams team asked Mario to stand in for the US West Grand Prix in Long Beach. Mario qualified 14th fastest, but retired from the race due to accident damage to his Williams-Ford.

For Ferrari, 1982 was a tragic season. Gilles Villeneuve was killed in qualifying for the Belgian Grand Prix, and when Didier Pironi was severely injured in practice for the German Grand Prix, the Italians asked Mario to drive for them in the final two Grands Prix of the year at Monza (Italy, photo) and Las Vegas (USA).

For Mario, it was an emotional return to Ferrari and Monza. Sensationally, he qualified in pole position (photo), and in the race he finished in third place. The four points from Mario's third place (and the six points from teammate Patrick Tambay's second place) secured the 1982 Constructors' World Championship for Ferrari.

Part Two:
Mario Andretti's
Career outside Formula One

Mario Andretti is the greatest all-rounder to have won the Formula One World Championship. He competed successfully in several very different forms of racing including ChampCar, NASCAR and sport-protypes. Here Mario and co-driver Jacky Ickx celebrate one of their four wins for Ferrari in the 1972 World Sports Car Championship.

Mario is one of the most successful drivers in the history of ChampCars, but he only won the Indy 500 one time in 1969. He started practice in this new 4wd Lotus-Ford 64 and was a frontrunner for most of May, but then destroyed the car in a crash shortly before the race. This meant he had to drive his spare car, the older Hawke-Ford.

Despite the practice crash and the fact that he was not running the newer and preferred Lotus, Mario went on to win the 1969 Indy 500 in this Hawke-Ford. 1969 was a great year for Mario as he won eight more ChampCar races and the ChampCar title. It was Mario's third ChampCar title, and he was to win the championship again in 1984.

Mario, still wearing the laurels from his Indy 500 win of 1969, on the victory lap around the circuit in the pace car. Mario, busy telling the spectators about the race in the microphone, is sitting on the shoulders of his team boss, STP Racing's Andy Granatelli. To the left of Mario, his wife Dee Ann looks on.

Mario's first win for Ferrari in the World Sports Car Championship came in the Sebring 12 Hour race in 1970. He shared a Ferrari 512S with Italians Ignazio Giunti and Nino Vaccarella. Photo shows Mario (left) celebrating after the race with Giunti (center) and Vaccarella.

Mario in the Ferrari 512S in the 1970 Watkins Glen 6 Hours race. He again shared the car with fellow-Sebring 12 Hour race winner Ignazio Giunti, a talented Italian who was killed in the beginning of 1971 in a sports car race at the Buenos Aires Autodromo in Argentina.

Following his win in 1969, Mario had number 1 on his car for the 1970 Indy 500. The car was a McNamara, but one car was almost written off in a crash during qualifying. Mario eventually qualified for the third row, but any hopes of repeating the 1969 win disappeared when the car began to handle erratically, and he only finished sixth.

1972 was a successful year for Mario Andretti in the World Sports Car Championship. With Jacky Ickx as his co-driver in the Ferrari team, Mario won four races including both the American classics, Sebring 12 Hour and Daytona. Photo shows Mario leading Ferrari teammates Clay Regazzoni (4) and Ronnie Peterson (3) at Sebring.

Mario and Jacky Ickx also took their Ferrari to first place in the Brands Hatch round of the World Sports Car Championship in 1972. Photo shows Mario accelerating out of the Druids hairpin in the Ferrari. Jacky Ickx is the most successful driver in the Le Mans 24 Hour race ever, but Mario never managed to win the French endurance race.

Mario only won the Indy 500 once, but he was usually a frontrunner at the "Brickyard" from his debut in the mid-1960s to his retirement from single-seaters in 1994. Mario (bottom) raced against American legends A. J. Foyt (left), Gordon Johncock (middle, top), Johnny Rutherford (middle, bottom), Al Unser (right, top) and Bobby Unser (right, center).

The International Race Of Champions (IROC), a series of races where stars from different categories in motor racing compete against each other in identical cars, often had Mario on the entry list, and he won the championship in 1979. Here Mario, third from right, poses with the IROC line-up a couple of years earlier at Michigan International Speedway.

In 1988 Mario drove a Porsche 962C in the 24 Hour Le Mans race in France. His co-drivers were son Michael and nephew John, and the Andretti family team finished in sixth position. Five years earlier Mario and Michael had finished third in Le Mans in a Porsche 956 partnered by France's Philippe Alliot.

Mario and nephew, John Andretti (right), in the pits during the 1988 24 Hour race at Le Mans. John went on to become a winner in ChampCar racing, but was never as successful as Mario's son Michael, who was one of the superstars of ChampCar racing in the 1990s. John later switched to the NASCAR series.

Mario (center) with son Michael (left) and nephew John. The trio made ChampCar history in the 1991 race in Milwaukee when Michael won in front of John and Mario. The "All Andretti Podium" came in a season which saw Mario finish seventh in the ChampCar championship with a second place as his best race result.

In the late 1980s Mario raced a Porsche 962C in sports prototype events, and sometimes shared the car with son Michael and nephew John. Photo shows Mario testing the American version of the Porsche sponsored by Texaco Havoline and on BF Goodrich tires. Mario took part in the 1988 Le Mans with Michael and John in a Shell sponsored Porsche 962C.

Mario during the 1994 Indy 500. It was his final race at the famous Indiana speedway, and he qualified ninth, but retired from the race. In his ChampCar career, Mario started in 29 races at "The Brickyard," which gave him second place on the list of Indy 500 starts. Only A. J. Foyt, with 35 starts, has more Indy 500 experience.

1994 was Mario Andretti's final year in ChampCar racing. His season was titled the "Arrividerci, Mario" tour, and in his Newman-Haas Lola T93 (photo), he scored one third place on his way to 14th position in the championship. Mario's teammate during his last ChampCar season was 1992 Formula One World Champion Nigel Mansell.

For 1995 Mario was a member of Porsche's star-studded factory team for the Daytona 24 Hour race, and he completed almost 5000 trouble-free kilometers in testing in the car, which was built by Tom Walkinshae Racing. Due to shock rule changes shortly before the race, Porsche pulled out and Mario never started the race.

Mario never won the 24 Hour race in Le Mans. His best result was second place in the 1995 race when he shared a Courage-Porsche with French veteran Bob Wollek (left) and young Frenchman Eric Helary. The following year Mario finished 13th in Le Mans in a Courage-Porsche with Derek Warwick and Jan Lammers. In his last Le Mans in 1997, he retired with accident damage to his Courage-Porsche.

Mario today, in the pit lane offering advice to his son Michael. After one of the longest and most successful careers in international racing, the checkered flag is finally out for Mario. But from the pits, the sport's greatest all-rounder still enjoys motor racing as much as ever...

Appendix A

Mario Andretti
Overall View

Personal details:
Born: February 28 1940 in Montona, Italy
Married to Dee Ann
Children: Michael, Jeff and Barbie
Debut in racing: 1959 at Nazareth Speedway
(USA) in 1948 Hudson Hornet

Formula One World Championship:
Years active: 1968 - 1982
Number of Grands Prix: 128
Number of wins: 12
Race-per-win ratio: 10.67
World Championship titles: 1 (1978)
Number of pole positions: 18
World Championship points: 180
Average number of points per Grand Prix: 1.41
Number of fastest laps: 10

Formula One World Championship Grand Prix Wins:
1971: South African Grand Prix (in Ferrari 312B)
1976: Japanese Grand Prix (in Lotus-Ford 77)
1977: USA West Grand Prix (in Lotus-Ford 78)
1977: Spanish Grand Prix (in Lotus-Ford 78)
1977: French Grand Prix (in Lotus-Ford 78)
1977: Italian Grand Prix (in Lotus-Ford 78)
1978: Argentinean Grand Prix (in Lotus-Ford 78)
1978: Belgian Grand Prix (in Lotus-Ford 79)
1978: Spanish Grand Prix (in Lotus-Ford 79)
1978: French Grand Prix (in Lotus-Ford 79)
1978: German Grand Prix (in Lotus-Ford 79)
1978: Dutch Grand Prix (in Lotus-Ford 79)

ChampCar:
Years active: 1964 - 1994
Number of races: 407 (all-time record)
Number of wins: 52
Championship titles: 4 (1965, 66, 69, 84)
Number of pole positions: 67 (all-time record)

Other Championships:
1974: USAC Dirt Track Champion

1979: IROC Champion

Other major race wins:
World Sport Car Championship:
1967: Sebring 12 Hours (in Ford Mark IV with Bruce McLaren as co-driver)
1970: Sebring 12 Hours (in Ferrari 512S with Ignazio Giunti and Nino Vaccarella as co-drivers)
1972: Daytona Six Hours, Sebring 12 Hours, Brands Hatch 1000 kms, Watkins Glen Six-Hours (all in Ferrari 312P and with Jacky Ickx as co-driver)
1974: Monza 1000 kms (in Alfa Romeo T33TT with Arturo Merzario as co-driver

---

NASCAR:
1967: Daytona 500 (in Ford 200)

USAC Sprint Car: 9 wins
USAC Midget Car: 1 win
USAC Dirt Car: 5 wins

Appendix B:

Mario Andretti's Formula One Career

1968:

Mario makes Formula One debut for Lotus in Italian Grand Prix at Monza - fastest in testing in the week leading up to the race - fastest in opening session but then leaves for Saturday's USAC Hoosier 100 race in Indiana, USA - banned from starting the Grand Prix on return to Monza as he has competed in another race within 24 hours - back in Formula One for US Grand Prix at Watkins Glen - takes pole position - first driver in Formula One history to take pole position for debut Grand Prix - runs second in opening stages of race but then retires with clutch problems.

Team: Gold Leaf Team Lotus
Teammate(s): Graham Hill, Jackie Oliver
Car: Lotus 49B
Engine: Ford Cosworth V-8
Number of Grands Prix entered: 2 (of 12)
Number of Grands Prix started: 1
Wins: -
2nd. places: -
3rd. places: -
4th. places: -
5th. places: -
6th. places: -
Finishes outside top-6: -
Retirements: 1
Accidents/left track (races only): -
Pole positions: 1
Best grid position: 1st.
Fastest lap in races: -
Points in World Championship: -
Position in World Championship:
Non-championship Formula One races: -
Best position in non-championship races: -

———————————————

1969:

Stays with Lotus in Formula One for sporadic season - closes dramatically on leaders in opening race of the year, South African Grand Prix, when transmission fails on his Lotus 49B - entered for Dutch Grand Prix but stays in USA for Langhorne 150 - switches to Lotus' experimental 63 4wd car for German Grand Prix but crashes out on first lap - retires from US Grand Prix in 63 4wd with suspension damage.

Team: Gold Leaf Team Lotus
Teammate(s): Graham Hill, Jochen Rindt
Car: Lotus 49B and Lotus 63 (4wd)
Engine: Ford Cosworth V-8 (both cars)
Number of Grands Prix entered: 4 (of 11)
Number of Grands Prix started: 3
Wins: -
2nd. places: -
3rd. places: -
4th. places: -
5th. places: -
6th. places: -
Finishes outside top-6: -
Retirements: 3
Accidents/left track (races only): 1
Pole positions: -
Best grid position: 6th.
Fastest lap in races: -
Points in World Championship: -
Position in World Championship:
Non-championship Formula One races: -
Best position in non-championship races: -

———————————————

1970:

Sponsor STP creates Formula One team with March chassis for Mario - still only sporadic Formula One season with five Grands Prix - entered for three more races but did not arrive - engine shortage hampers programme - March not competitive - finally finishes a Grand Prix in Spain and takes 3rd. place - escapes unhurt from dramatic crash in Austrian Grand Prix.

Team: STP Corporation
Teammate(s): - (one-car team)
Car: March 701
Engine: Ford Cosworth V-8
Number of Grands Prix entered: 8 (of 13)
Number of Grands Prix started: 5
Wins: -
2nd. places: -
3rd. places: 1
4th. places: -
5th. places: -
6th. places: -
Finishes outside top-6: -
Retirements: 4
Accidents/left track (races only): 1
Pole positions: -
Best grid position: 9th.
Fastest lap in races: -
Points in World Championship: 4
Position in World Championship: 15th.
Non-championship Formula One races: -
Best position in non-championship races: -

1971:

Mario signs with Ferrari for both sports cars and Formula One - takes part in only five of 11 Grands Prix - entered for four more but did not arrive - begins season in Ferrari 312B - wins debut race for Ferrari in South African Grand Prix and sets fastest lap - also wins second Formula One race for Ferrari, non-championship US West Grand Prix at Ontario - did not qualify for Monaco Grand Prix due to engine problems in only dry session - non-starter in non-championship Rhein Pokalrennen at Hockenheim as he was suffering from hands burned in USAC race incident - switched to Ferrari 312B2 from German Grand Prix - qualified 6th. for US Grand Prix but did not start due to USAC commitment in Trenton.

Team: Spa Ferrari SEFAC
Teammate(s): Jacky Ickx, Clay Regazzoni
Car: Ferrari 312B and Ferrari 313B2
Engine: Ferrari V-12 (both cars)
Number of Grands Prix entered: 9 (of 11)
Number of Grands Prix started: 5
Wins: 1
2nd. places: -
3rd. places: -
4th. places: 1
5th. places: -
6th. places: -
Finishes outside top-6: 1
Retirements: 2
Accidents/left track (races only): -
Pole positions: -
Best grid position: 4th.
Fastest lap in races: 1
Points in World Championship: 12
Position in World Championship: 8th.
Non-championship Formula One races: 1
Best position in non-championship races: 1st. (United States West G. P., Ontario)

1972:

Mario stays with Ferrari for another sporadic Formula One season - entered for seven of the 12 Grands Prix but only starts in five - qualifies in top-10 for all five Grands Prix but best result is 4th. in South Africa - stops in Formula One to concentrate on American career in 1973 and most of 1974.

Team: Spa Ferrari SEFAC
Teammate(s): Jacky Ickx, Clay Regazzoni, Nanni Galli, Arturo Merzario
Car: Ferrari 312B2
Engine: Ferrari V-12
Number of Grands Prix entered: 7 (of 12)
Number of Grands Prix started: 5
Wins: -
2nd. places: -
3rd. places: -
4th. places: 1
5th. places: -
6th. places: 1
Finishes outside top-6: 1
Retirements: 2
Accidents/left track (races only): -
Pole positions: -
Best grid position: 5th.
Fastest lap in races: -
Points in World Championship: 4
Position in World Championship: 12th.
Non-championship Formula One races: -
Best position in non-championship races: -

1974:
Mario makes Formula One comeback for American Vel's Parnelli Jones team - only takes part in final two Grands Prix of season - qualifies 16th. for Parnelli Jones' first For-

mula One race in Canada but stalls on the grid - qualifies strong 3rd. fastest for US Grand Prix but is disqualified after push start on grid.

Team: Vel's Parnelli Jones Racing
Teammate(s): - (one-car team)
Car: Parnelli VPJ4
Engine: Ford Cosworth V-8
Number of Grands Prix entered: 2 (of 15)
Number of Grands Prix started: 2
Wins: -
2nd. places: -
3rd. places: -
4th. places: -
5th. places: -
6th. places: -
Finishes outside top-6: 1
Retirements: 1
Accidents/left track (races only): -
Pole positions: -
Best grid position: 3rd.
Fastest lap in races: -
Points in World Championship: -
Position in World Championship: -
Non-championship Formula One races: -
Best position in non-championship races: -

1975:
Mario stays with Vel's Parnelli Jones for almost full Formula One season - misses Belgian Grand Prix due to Indy 500 commitments in USA - also misses Dutch Grand Prix due to

ChampCar commitment - strong race in Spain from 4th. on grid and fastest lap but crashes out while leading - scores Parnelli Jones' first Formula One points with fourth place in Sweden - also fifth in French Grand Prix.

Team: Vel's Parnelli Jones Racing
Teammate(s): - (one-car team)
Car: Parnelli VPJ4
Engine: Ford Cosworth V-8
Number of Grands Prix entered: 12 (of 14)
Number of Grands Prix started: 12
Wins: -
2nd. places: -
3rd. places: -
4th. places: 1
5th. places: 1
6th. places: -
Finishes outside top-6: 4
Retirements: 6
Accidents/left track (races only): 2
Pole positions: -
Best grid position: 4th.
Fastest lap in races: 1
Points in World Championship: 5
Position in World Championship: 14th.
Non-championship Formula One races: 1
Best position in non-championship races: 3rd. (International Trophy, Silverstone)

1976:
Mario starts the season with Lotus

and crashes with new team mate Ronnie Peterson in opening race in Brazil - goes back to Vel's Parnelli Jones when team makes come-back in South Africa - takes sixth place in South Africa - drives for Wolf-Williams in non-championship International Trophy at Silverstone when Vel's Parnelli Jones leaves Formula One after only two races - returns to Lotus for Spanish Grand Prix and rest of season - misses Monaco Grand Prix due to Indy 500 commitments - Lotus 77 gradually improves - Mario qualifies second and sets fastest lap but retires in Swedish Grand Prix - finishes third in Dutch and Canadian Grands Prix - finishes season with pole position and win in Japan.
Team: John Player Team Lotus (13 races), Val's Parnelli Jones Racing (2 races)
Teammate(s): Lotus: Ronnie Peterson, Gunnar Nilsson / Parnelli: -
Car: Lotus 77, Parnelli VPJ4B
Engine: Ford Cosworth V-8 (both cars)
Number of Grands Prix entered: 15 (of 16)
Number of Grands Prix started: 15
Wins: 1
2nd. places: -
3rd. places: 2
4th. places: -
5th. places: 2
6th. places: 1
Finishes outside top-6: 1
Retirements: 8
Accidents/left track (races only): 2
Pole positions: 1
Best grid position: 1st.
Fastest lap in races: -
Points in World Championship: 2
Position in World Championship: 6th.
Non-championship Formula One races: 1
Best position in non-championship races: 7th. (International Trophy, Silverstone)

1977:
Mario finally concentrates on Formula One and has full season with Lotus - Lotus 78 gradually becomes the fastest car of the season - qualifies second and leads non-championship Race of Champions before retiring - Mario wins US (West), Spanish, French and Italian Grands Prix - sets fastest lap in Sweden, France, Italy and Canada - takes pole position in Spain, Belgium, Sweden, France, Holland, Canada and Japan - engine problems in four races in a row at mid-season cost Mario all chances of winning the championship - Niki Lauda wins championship in Ferrari with three wins to Mario's four.
Team: John Player Team Lotus
Teammate(s): Gunnar Nilsson
Car: Lotus 78
Engine: Ford Cosworth V-8
Number of Grands Prix entered: 17 (of 17)
Number of Grands Prix started: 17
Wins: 4
2nd. places: 1
3rd. places: -
4th. places: -
5th. places: 2
6th. places: 1
Finishes outside top-6: 1
Retirements: 8
Accidents/left track (races only): 2
Pole positions: 7
Best grid position: 1st.
Fastest lap in races: 4
Points in World Championship: 47
Position in World Championship: 3rd.
Non-championship Formula One races: 1
Best position in non-championship races: (retired)

1978:
Mario starts season in Lotus 78 and wins season-opener in Argentina from pole position - crashes out of lead in non-championship race International Trophy - switches to new Lotus 79 for Belgian Grand Prix - Lotus 79 in a class of its own - Mario wins Belgian, Spanish, French, German and Dutch Grands Prix to take World Championship - takes pole position in Argentina, Belgium, Spain, Sweden, Ger-

many, Holland, Italy and US East - sets fastest lap in South Africa, Spain and Italy - teammate, close friend and only title rival, Ronnie Peterson killed in Italian Grand Prix - Mario clinches title with sixth place in Italian Grand Prix - crosses the line first but is penalized one minute for jumping the start.

Team: John Player Team Lotus
Team mate(s): Ronnie Peterson, Jean-Pierre Jarier
Car: Lotus 78 and Lotus 79
Engine: Ford Cosworth V-8 (both cars)
Number of Grands Prix entered: 16 (of 16)
Number of Grands Prix started: 16
Wins: 6
2nd. places: 1
3rd. places: -
4th. places: 1
5th. places: -
6th. places: 1
Finishes outside top-6: 3
Retirements: 4
Accidents/left track (races only): 1
Pole positions: 8
Best grid position: 1st.
Fastest lap in races: 3
Points in World Championship: 64
Position in World Championship: WORLD CHAMPION
Non-championship Formula One races: 1

Best position in non-championship races: (retired)

1979:

Mario stays with Lotus for title defence - starts season in Lotus 79 - Lotus 79 overtaken by rivals Ligier, Ferrari and Williams - successor Lotus 80 introduced for Spanish Grand Prix but not competitive - returns to Lotus 79 for Belgian Grand Prix - drives Lotus 80 in Monaco and French Grands Prix - then returns to Lotus 79 for rest of season - best result is third place in Spain - qualifies on pole position for non-championship Race of Champions and finishes third.

Team: Martini Racing Team Lotus
Teammate(s): Carlos Reutemann
Car: Lotus 79 and Lotus 80
Engine: Ford Cosworth V-8 (both cars)
Number of Grands Prix entered: 15 (of 15)
Number of Grands Prix started: 15
Wins: -
2nd. places: -
3rd. places: 1
4th. places: 2
5th. places: 2
6th. places: -
Finishes outside top-6: 1
Retirements: 9
Accidents/left track (races only): -
Pole positions: -

Best grid position: 4th.
Fastest lap in races: -
Points in World Championship: 14
Position in World Championship: 10th.
Non-championship Formula One races: 1
Best position in non-championship races: 3rd. (Race of Champions, Brands Hatch)

1980:

Mario stays with Lotus - new Lotus 81 neither reliable nor competitive - qualifies sixth for season-opener in Argentina - scores only a single point in final race of the year; US East Grand Prix - also races in Spanish Grand Prix which becomes a non-championship race because of "political problems."

Team: Team Essex Lotus
Teammate(s): Elio de Angelis, Nigel Mansell
Car: Lotus 81
Engine: Ford Cosworth V-8
Number of Grands Prix entered: 14 (of 14)
Number of Grands Prix started: 14
Wins: -
2nd. places: -
3rd. places: -
4th. places: -
5th. places: -
6th. places: 1

Finishes outside top-6: 4
Retirements: 9
Accidents/left track (races only): 2
Pole positions: -
Best grid position: 6th.
Fastest lap in races: -
Points in World Championship: 1
Position in World Championship: 20th.
Non-championship Formula One races: 1
Best position in non-championship races: (retired)

1981:

Mario signs with Alfa Romeo for final, full Formula One year - season starts well with sixth on the grid and fourth place in the US West Grand Prix - Mario rarely qualifies in top-10 and scores no points in the rest of the season.

Team: Marlboro Team Alfa Romeo
Teammate(s): Bruno Giacomelli
Car: Alfa Romeo 179C
Engine: Alfa Romeo V-12
Number of Grands Prix entered: 15 (of 15)
Number of Grands Prix started: 15
Wins: -
2nd. places: -
3rd. places: -
4th. places: 1
5th. places: -
6th. places: -

Finishes outside top-6: 6
Retirements: 8
Accidents/left track (races only): 3
Pole positions: -
Best grid position: 6th.
Fastest lap in races: -
Points in World Championship: 3
Position in World Championship: 17th.
Non-championship Formula One races: -
Best position in non-championship races: -

1982:

Mario concentrates on ChampCar racing - is invited to stand-in for the suddenly retired Carlos Reutemann in Williams team for US West Grand Prix - qualifies 14th. but retires early with accident damage - is invited to stand-in for the injured Didier Pironi in Ferrari team for Italian and US Las Vegas Grands Prix - takes pole for Italian Grand Prix at Monza and finishes third - Mario's third place at Monza clinches Constructors' Championship for Ferrari - Mario's Formula One career ends when the Ferrari's rear suspension collapses on lap 26 of the US Las Vegas Grand Prix - Mario is running sixth at the time; just in front of Keke Rosberg, who later that afternoon clinches the 1982 World Championship.

Team: TAG Williams Team (1 race), Scuderia Ferrari SPA SEFAC (2 races)
Teammate(s): Williams: Keke Rosberg / Ferrari: Patrick Tambay
Car: Williams FW07C, Ferrari 126C2
Engine: Ford Cosworth V-8 (Williams) and Ferrari V-6 turbo (Ferrari)
Number of Grands Prix entered: 3 (of 16)
Number of Grands Prix started: 3
Wins: -
2nd. places: -
3rd. places: 1
4th. places: -
5th. places: -
6th. places: -
Finishes outside top-6: -
Retirements: 2
Accidents/left track (races only): 1
Pole positions: 1
Best grid position: 1st.
Fastest lap in races: 1
Points in World Championship: 4
Position in World Championship: 19th.
Non-championship Formula One races: -
Best position in non-championship races:

Appendix C:

Mario Andretti's
Career outside Formula One

1959: Debut at Nazareth Speedway in 1948 Hudson Hornet.

1964: First ChampCar race at Trenton (finished 11th.) - third in Sprint Car Championship.

1965: ChampCar champion with one win - wins first ChampCar race (Hoosier Grand Prix) - starts fourth and finishes third in Indy 500 - Indianapolis Rookie of the Year - named "Fans' Driver of the Year."

1966: ChampCar champion with eight wins - pole position for Indy 500 but retires - wins five sprint car races and finishes second in championship - makes Le Mans debut in Ford Mrk2 but retires - receives Ford Award as the "Man Who Has Done Most for Auto Racing in 1966."

1967: Eight ChampCar wins - loses win and championship in final race with pitstop three laps from finish - pole position for Indy 500 but retires - named "Driver of the Year" - wins Sebring (World Sport Car Championship) - wins Daytona 500 (NASCAR) - retires from Le Mans (in Ford Mrk4).

1968: Four ChampCar wins - again loses title in final race - starts fourth for Indy 500 but retires.

1969: ChampCar champion with nine wins - starts second and wins Indy 500 - second in Sebring 12 Hours with Ferrari - 13th. in Can-Am Championship.

1970: One ChampCar win - fifth in ChampCar Championship - starts eight and finishes sixth in Indy 500 - wins Sebring (World Sport Car Championship) - qualifies on pole position for Daytona 24 Hours and finishes third for Ferrari.

1971: No ChampCar wins - ninth in ChampCar Championship - starts ninth for Indy 500 but retires.

1972: No ChampCar wins - starts fifth and is classified eight in Indy 500 - wins Daytona, Sebring, Brands Hatch and Watkins Glen (World Sport Car Championship).

1973: One ChampCar win - fifth in ChampCar Championship - starts sixth for Indy 500 but retires.

1974: No ChampCar wins - starts fifth for Indy 500 but retires - wins Monza (World Sport Car Championship) - three wins in SCCA/USAC Formula 5000 Championship - second SCCA/USAC Formula 5000 Championship - wins USAC Dirt Track Championship.

1975: No ChampCar wins - starts 27th. for Indy 500 but retires - four wins in SCCA/USAC Formula 5000 Championship - second in SCCA/USAC Formula 5000 Championship.

1976: No ChampCar wins - ninth in ChampCar Championship - starts 19th. for Indy 500 and is classified eight.

1977: No ChampCar win - seventh in ChampCar Championship - starts sixth for Indy 500 but retires.

1978: One ChampCar win - 17th. in ChampCar Championship - starts 33rd. for Indy 500 and finishes 12th - named "Driver of the Year."

1979: Concentrates on Formula One

- One ChampCar race (3rd. in Ontario) - wins IROC series.

1980: One ChampCar win - 16th. in ChampCar Championship - starts second for Indy 500 but retires - fifth in IROC series.

1981: No ChampCar wins (best position: Second) - 11th. in ChampCar Championship - starts 32nd. and finishes second in Indy 500 - proclaimed winner due to one-lap penalty to first-place finisher Bobby Unser - relegated to second place when win was given back to Unser in October.

1982: No ChampCar wins (best position: Second) - third in ChampCar Championship - starts fourth for Indy 500 but retires - banned from starting Le Mans with son Michael in Mirage M12 due to illegal position of oil cooler.

1983: Two ChampCar wins - third in ChampCar Championship - starts 11th. for Indy 500 but retires - third in Le Mans with son Michael and Philippe Alliot in Porsche 956.

1984: ChampCar champion with six wins - starts sixth for Indy 500 but retires - named "Driver of the "Year."

1985: Three ChampCar wins - fifth in ChampCar Championship - starts fourth and finishes second in Indy 500 - injured in Michigan 500 and misses following race.

1986: Two ChampCar wins - seventh in ChampCar Championship - earns closest margin of victory in ChampCar racing in Portland on Father's Day by beating son Michael by 0,07 seconds - starts 30th. for Indy 500 but retires.

1987: Two ChampCar wins - sixth in Champcar Championship - pole position for Indy 500 but retires.

1988: Two ChampCar wins - fifth in ChampCar Championship - starts fourth for Indy 500 but retires - sixth in Le Mans with son Michael and nephew John in Porsche 962C.

1989: Joins son Michael at Newman-Haas ChampCar team - no ChampCar wins (best position: Second) - sixth in ChampCar Championship - starts fifth and finishes fourth for Indy 500.

1990: No ChampCar wins (best position: Second) - seventh in ChampCar Championship - starts sixth for Indy 500 but retires.

1991: No ChampCar wins (best position: Second) - joins son Michael (winner) and nephew John (second) on Milwaukee podium - seventh in ChampCar Championship - starts third and finishes seventh in Indy 500.

1992: No ChampCar wins (best position: Second) - sixth in ChampCar Championship - starts third for Indy 500 but crashes out and breaks toes on both feet - named "Driver of Quarter Century."

1993: One ChampCar win - sets world closed-course speed record at Michigan with speed of 377,03 km/h - sixth in ChampCar Championship – starts second and finishes fifth in Indy 500.

1994: No ChampCar win (best position: Third) - 14th. in Champcar Championship -

qualifies ninth for Indy 500 but retires - stops ChampCar racing after "Arrivederci, Mario" tour.

1995: Finishes second in Le Mans with Bob Wollek and Eric Helary in Courage-Porsche.

1996: Finishes 13th. in Le Mans with Derek Warwick and Jan Lammers in Courage Porsche C36.

1997: Retires with accident damage from Le Mans with son Michael and Olivier Grouillard in Courage C36.

Appendix D:

Mario Andretti's
World Championship Cars

In his World Championship year 1978, Mario Andretti drove two cars: The Lotus 78 (from 1977) and the all-new Lotus 79.

Lotus 78:
Used for 5 races (round 1 - 5)
Designer(s): Colin Chapman, Ralph Bellamy
Chassis: Full monocoque
Engine: Ford Cosworth V-6
Bore x stroke: 85,7 x 64,8 mm
Capacity: 2993 ccm
Output: App. 485 bhp
Gearbox: Hewland 5-speed
Tyres: Goodyear
Weight: App. 588 kg

Lotus 79:
Used for 11 races (round 6 - 16)
Designer(s): Colin Chapman, Martin Ogilvie
Chassis: Full monocoque
Engine: Ford Cosworth V-8
Bore x stroke: 85,7 x 64,8 mm
Capacity: 2993 ccm
Output: App. 485 bhp
Gearbox: Hewland 5- and 6-speed
Tyres: Goodyear
Weight: App. 575 kg

More Titles from Iconografix:

AMERICAN CULTURE
AMERICAN SERVICE STATIONS 1935-1943
ISBN 1-882256-27-1
COCA-COLA: A HISTORY IN PHOTOGRAPHS 1930-1969
ISBN 1-882256-46-8
COCA-COLA: ITS VEHICLES IN PHOTOGRAPHS 1930-1969
ISBN 1-882256-47-6
PHILLIPS 66 1945-1954   ISBN 1-882256-42-5

AUTOMOTIVE
CADILLAC 1948-1964   ISBN 1-882256-83-2
CORVETTE PROTOTYPES & SHOW CARS
ISBN 1-882256-77-8
EARLY FORD V-8S 1932-1942 ISBN 1-882256-97-2
FERRARI PININFARINA 1952-1996 ISBN 1-882256-65-4
IMPERIAL 1955-1963   ISBN 1-882256-22-0
IMPERIAL 1964-1968   ISBN 1-882256-23-9
LINCOLN MOTOR CARS 1920-1942 ISBN 1-882256-57-3
LINCOLN MOTOR CARS 1946-1960 ISBN 1-882256-58-1
PACKARD MOTOR CARS 1935-1942 ISBN 1-882256-44-1
PACKARD MOTOR CARS 1946-1958 ISBN 1-882256-45-X
PLYMOUTH COMMERCIAL VEHICLES
ISBN 1-58388-004-6
PONTIAC DREAM CARS, SHOW CARS & PROTOTYPES
1928-1998   ISBN 1-882256-93-X
PONTIAC FIREBIRD TRANS-AM 1969-1999
ISBN 1-882256-95-6
PORSCHE 356 1948-1965   ISBN 1-882256-85-9
STUDEBAKER 1933-1942   ISBN 1-882256-24-7
STUDEBAKER 1946-1958   ISBN 1-882256-25-5

EMERGENCY VEHICLES
AMERICAN LAFRANCE 700 SERIES 1945-1952
ISBN 1-882256-90-5
AMERICAN LAFRANCE 700&800 SERIES 1953-1958
ISBN 1-882256-91-3
AMERICAN LAFRANCE 900 SERIES 1958-1964
ISBN 1-58388-002-X
CLASSIC AMERICAN AMBULANCES 1900-1979
ISBN 1-882256-94-8
FIRE CHIEF CARS 1900-1997 ISBN 1-882256-87-5
MACK® MODEL B FIRE TRUCKS 1954-1966*
ISBN 1-882256-62-X
MACK MODEL CF FIRE TRUCKS 1967-1981*
ISBN 1-882256-63-8
MACK MODEL L FIRE TRUCKS 1940-1954*
ISBN 1-882256-86-7
SEAGRAVE 70TH ANNIVERSARY SERIES
ISBN 1-58388-001-1
VOLUNTEER & RURAL FIRE APPARATUS
ISBN 1-58388-005-4

PUBLIC TRANSIT
THE GENERAL MOTORS NEW LOOK BUS
ISBN 1-58388-007-0

RACING
GT40   ISBN 1-882256-64-6
JUAN MANUEL FANGIO WORLD CHAMPION DRIVER SERIES
ISBN 1-58388-008-9
LE MANS 1950: THE BRIGGS CUNNINGHAM
CAMPAIGN   ISBN 1-882256-21-2
LOLA RACE CARS 1962-1990 ISBN 1-882256-73-5
LOTUS RACE CARS 1961-1994 ISBN 1-882256-84-0
MARIO ANDRETTI WORLD CHAMPION DRIVER SERIES
ISBN 1-58388-009-7
MCLAREN RACE CARS 1965-1996 ISBN 1-882256-74-3
SEBRING 12-HOUR RACE 1970 ISBN 1-882256-20-4
VANDERBILT CUP RACE 1936 & 1937
ISBN 1-882256-66-2
WILLIAMS 1969-1999 30 YEARS OF GRAND PRIX RACING
ISBN 1-58388-000-3

RAILWAYS
CHICAGO, ST. PAUL, MINNEAPOLIS & OMAHA RAILWAY
1880-1940   ISBN 1-882256-67-0
CHICAGO&NORTH WESTERN RAILWAY 1975-1995
ISBN 1-882256-76-X
GREAT NORTHERN RAILWAY 1945-1970
ISBN 1-882256-56-5
GREAT NORTHERN RAILWAY 1945-1970 VOLUME 2
ISBN 1-882256-79-4
MILWAUKEE ROAD 1850-1960 ISBN 1-882256-61-1
SOO LINE 1975-1992   ISBN 1-882256-68-9
TRAINS OF THE TWIN PORTS, DULUTH-SUPERIOR IN THE
1950s   ISBN 1-58388-003-8
WISCONSIN CENTRAL LIMITED 1987-1996
ISBN 1-882256-75-1
WISCONSIN CENTRAL RAILWAY 1871-1909
ISBN 1-882256-78-6

TRUCKS
BEVERAGE TRUCKS 1910-1975 ISBN 1-882256-60-3
BROCKWAY TRUCKS 1948-1961* ISBN 1-882256-55-7
DODGE PICKUPS 1939-1978 ISBN 1-882256-82-4
DODGE POWER WAGONS 1940-1980 ISBN 1-882256-89-1
DODGE TRUCKS 1929-1947 ISBN 1-882256-36-0
DODGE TRUCKS 1948-1960 ISBN 1-882256-37-9
LOGGING TRUCKS 1915-1970 ISBN 1-882256-59-X
MACK MODEL AB*   ISBN 1-882256-18-2
MACK AP SUPER-DUTY TRUCKS 1926-1938*
ISBN 1-882256-54-9
MACK MODEL B 1953-1966 VOL 1* ISBN 1-882256-19-0

MACK MODEL B 1953-1966 VOL 2* ISBN 1-882256-34-4
MACK EB-EC-ED-EE-EF-EG-DE 1936-1951*
ISBN 1-882256-29-8
MACK EH-EJ-EM-EQ-ER-ES 1936-1950*
ISBN 1-882256-39-5
MACK FC-FCSW-NW 1936-1947* ISBN 1-882256-28-X
MACK FG-FH-FJ-FK-FN-FP-FT-FW 1937-1950*
ISBN 1-882256-35-2
MACK LF-LH-LJ-LM-LT 1940-1956* ISBN 1-882256-38-7
MACK TRUCKS PHOTO GALLERY* ISBN 1-882256-88-3
NEW CAR CARRIERS 1910-1998 ISBN 1-882256-98-0
STUDEBAKER TRUCKS 1927-1940 ISBN 1-882256-40-9
STUDEBAKER TRUCKS 1941-1964 ISBN 1-882256-41-7
WHITE TRUCKS 1900-1937 ISBN 1-882256-80-8

TRACTORS & CONSTRUCTION EQUIPMENT
CASE TRACTORS 1912-1959   ISBN 1-882256-32-8
CATERPILLAR THIRTY 2ND EDITION INCLUDING BEST
THIRTY 6G THIRTY & R-4   ISBN 1-58388-006-2
CATERPILLAR D-2 & R-2   ISBN 1-882256-99-9
CATERPILLAR D-8 1933-1974 INCLUDING DIESEL 75
ISBN 1-882256-96-4
CATERPILLAR MILITARY TRACTORS VOLUME 1
ISBN 1-882256-16-6
CATERPILLAR MILITARY TRACTORS VOLUME 2
ISBN 1-882256-17-4
CATERPILLAR SIXTY   ISBN 1-882256-05-0
CATERPILLAR PHOTO GALLERY ISBN 1-882256-70-0
CLETRAC AND OLIVER CRAWLERS ISBN 1-882256-43-3
ERIE SHOVEL   ISBN 1-882256-69-7
FARMALL CUB   ISBN 1-882256-71-9
FARMALL F- SERIES   ISBN 1-882256-02-6
FARMALL MODEL H   ISBN 1-882256-03-4
FARMALL MODEL M   ISBN 1-882256-15-8
FARMALL REGULAR   ISBN 1-882256-14-X
FARMALL SUPER SERIES   ISBN 1-882256-49-2
FORDSON 1917-1928   ISBN 1-882256-33-6
HART-PARR   ISBN 1-882256-08-5
HOLT TRACTORS   ISBN 1-882256-10-7
INTERNATIONAL TRACTRACTOR ISBN 1-882256-48-4
INTERNATIONAL TD CRAWLERS 1933-1962
ISBN 1-882256-72-7
JOHN DEERE MODEL A   ISBN 1-882256-12-3
JOHN DEERE MODEL B   ISBN 1-882256-01-8
JOHN DEERE MODEL D   ISBN 1-882256-00-X
JOHN DEERE 30 SERIES   ISBN 1-882256-13-1
MINNEAPOLIS-MOLINE U-SERIES ISBN 1-882256-07-7
OLIVER TRACTORS   ISBN 1-882256-09-3
RUSSELL GRADERS   ISBN 1-882256-11-5
TWIN CITY TRACTOR   ISBN 1-882256-06-9

*This product is sold under license from Mack Trucks, Inc. Mack is a registered Trademark of Mack Trucks, Inc. All rights reserved.

All Iconografix books are available from direct mail specialty book dealers and bookstores worldwide, or can be ordered from the publisher. For book trade and distribution information or to add your name to our mailing list contact

Iconografix
PO Box 446
Hudson, Wisconsin, 54016

Telephone: (715) 381-9755
(800) 289-3504 (USA)
Fax: (715) 381-9756

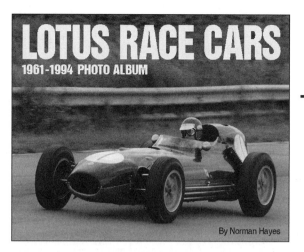

LOTUS RACE CARS
1961-1994 PHOTO ALBUM

By Norman Hayes

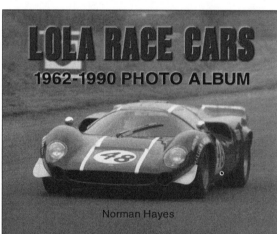

LOLA RACE CARS
1962-1990 PHOTO ALBUM

Norman Hayes

MORE GREAT BOOKS FROM ICONOGRAFIX

LOTUS RACE CARS 1961-1994 Photo Album   ISBN 1-882256-84-0

McLAREN RACE CARS 1965-1995 Photo Album   ISBN 1-882256-74-3

LOLA RACE CARS 1962-1990 Photo Album   ISBN 1-882256-73-5

LEMANS 1950 Photo Archive The Briggs Cunningham Campaign   ISBN 1-882256-21-2

WILLIAMS 1969-1998 Photo Album   ISBN 1-58388-00-3

JUAN MANUEL FANGIO World Champion Driver Series   ISBN 1-58388-008-9

SEBRING 12 HOUR RACE 1970 Photo Archive   ISBN 1-882256-20-4

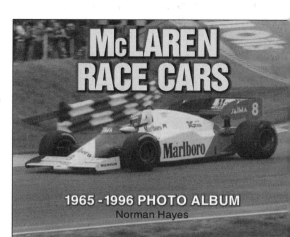

McLAREN RACE CARS
1965 - 1996 PHOTO ALBUM
Norman Hayes

LE MANS 1950 PHOTO ARCHIVE
The Briggs Cunningham Campaign

Edited with introduction by Robert C. Auten • Photographs by Smith Hempstone Oliver

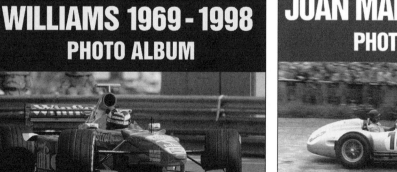

WILLIAMS 1969 - 1998
PHOTO ALBUM

30 YEARS OF GRAND PRIX RACING   Peter Nygaard

JUAN MANUEL FANGIO
PHOTO ALBUM

WORLD CHAMPION DRIVER SERIES
Peter Nygaard

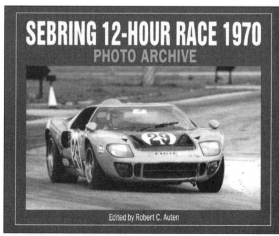

SEBRING 12-HOUR RACE 1970
PHOTO ARCHIVE

Edited by Robert C. Auten